4/15

Chris Paul

by Marty Gitlin

Consultant: Jon Krawczynski
AP Basketball Writer

BEARPORT
PUBLISHING

New York, New York

Credits

Cover and Title Page, © Damian Dovarganes/AP Images, Mark J. Terrill/AP Images, and Gerald Herbert/AP Images; 4, © Noah Graham/NBAE via Getty Images; 5, © Noah Graham/NBAE via Getty Images; 6, © Seth Poppel/Yearbook Library; 7, © Greg Fiume/Corbis; 8, © Jake Schoellkopf/AP Images; 9, © Jeff Glidden/AP Images; 10, © Greg Ashman/Icon Sportswire; 11, © Ty Russell/AP Images; 12, © Harry E. Walker/MCT/Newscom; 13, © Mark J. Terrill/AP Images; 14, © Danita Delimont/Alamy; 15, © Alex Brandon/AP Images; 16, © Chris Landsberger/AP Images; 17, © Bebeto Matthews/AP Images; 18, © Gerald Herbert/AP Images; 19, © Times-Picayune/Landov; 20, © Arnold Turner/Invision/AP Images; 21, © AP Images; 22L, © Staff/MCT/Newscom; 22R, © AP Images.

Publisher: Kenn Goin
Senior Editor: Joyce Tavolacci
Creative Director: Spencer Brinker
Photo Researcher: Chrös McDougall

Library of Congress Cataloging-in-Publication Data

Gitlin, Marty.
  Chris Paul / by Marty Gitlin.
    pages cm.—(Basketball heroes making a difference)
  Includes bibliographical references and index.
  ISBN 978-1-62724-547-0 (library binding)—ISBN 1-62724-547-2 (library binding)
  1. Paul, Chris, 1985–Juvenile literature. 2. Basketball players—United States—Biography—Juvenile literature. 3. Generosity—Juvenile literature. I. Title.
  GV884.P376G57 2015
  796.323092—dc23
  [B]
                    2014034560

For more information, write to Bearport Publishing Company, Inc., 45 West 21st Street, Suite 3B, New York, New York 10010. Printed in the United States of America.

10 9 8 7 6 5 4 3 2 1

Contents

Chris Comes Through

The Los Angeles Clippers were facing off against the Golden State Warriors on May 3, 2014. It was Game 7 of the first round of the **NBA playoffs**. The score was 87–84, with the Clippers leading, as the game neared the fourth quarter. Clippers **point guard** Chris Paul knew he needed to score big to nail down the victory for his team.

Despite the pressure, Chris kept his cool. With eight minutes left in the fourth quarter, he hit a **three-pointer**. One minute later, he used his amazing speed to dribble past two Warriors players to score on a **layup**. Chris then got two **assists**, and he made two late **free throws**. The Clippers won the game 126–121!

Chris drives to the hoop in Game 7 against the Warriors.

Chris (right) shoots against the Warriors during Game 7 of the 2014 playoffs.

In the NBA playoffs, the first team to win four games advances to the next round. If both teams win three games, the series comes down to an exciting Game 7, which determines the winner.

Growing Up

Years before he was sinking shots for the Clippers, Chris loved playing basketball and football with his older brother C.J. in his hometown of Winston-Salem, North Carolina. When not playing ball, Chris and C.J. could often be found at church or studying. Chris also spent many hours helping out at his grandfather's gas station.

In high school, Chris started to seriously focus on basketball. There was one problem, though. At five feet one inch (1.5 m), he was much shorter than the other basketball players. Chris, however, used his speed and quick thinking to become a star player despite his size. By the time he was a senior, he had shot up to six foot one (1.9 m)—and was one of the best players in the country.

Chris was the homecoming king at West Forsyth High School in Winston-Salem, North Carolina.

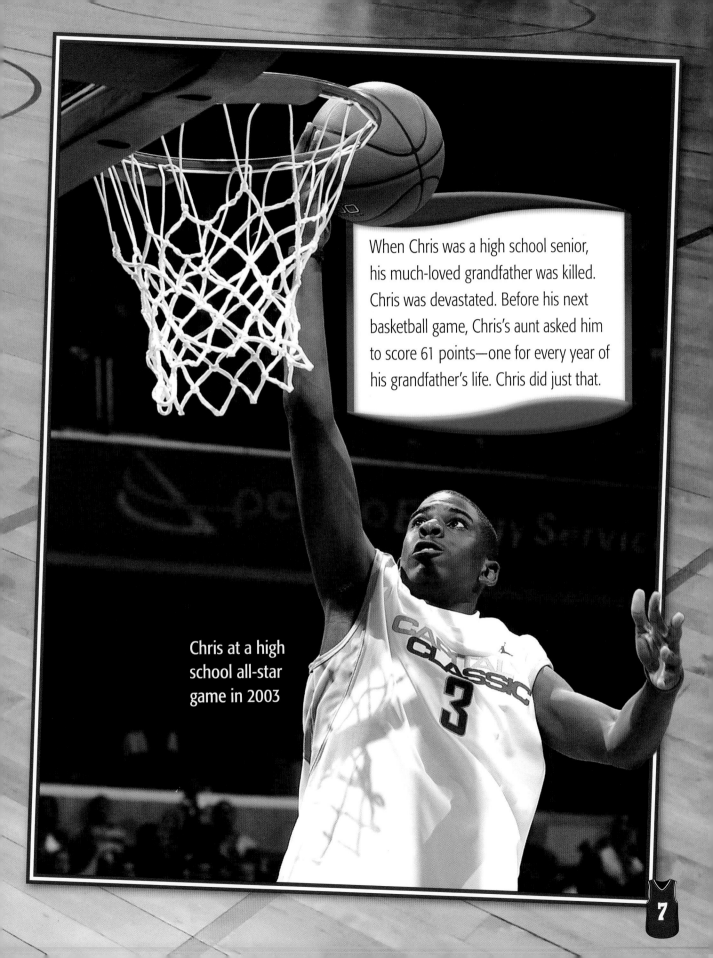

When Chris was a high school senior, his much-loved grandfather was killed. Chris was devastated. Before his next basketball game, Chris's aunt asked him to score 61 points—one for every year of his grandfather's life. Chris did just that.

Chris at a high school all-star game in 2003

Leading Wake Forest

When it was time for Chris to attend college, many schools tried to **recruit** him. Chris wanted to stay close to his family, though. So he decided to play for Wake Forest University in Winston-Salem.

As a point guard for Wake Forest's Demon Deacons, Chris was in charge of setting up the team's **offense**. The position was a great fit because Chris always seemed to know when and where to pass the ball, leading to lots of assists. Chris also developed into a great shooter. He was able to make baskets from anywhere on the court. Thanks to these amazing skills, Chris led Wake Forest to the **NCAA Tournament** twice. Then, after just two seasons, he decided it was time to follow his dream of playing in the NBA.

Chris was a star on the basketball court. He was also a good student, earning Academic All-America honors as a college sophomore.

In 2011, Wake Forest honored Chris by retiring his #3 jersey. That meant no other Wake Forest player could wear his uniform number.

Thanks to Chris, Wake Forest's basketball team was ranked number one in the country during the 2003–2004 season. The team had never before achieved that ranking.

The Top Rookie

In the 2005 NBA **draft**, the New Orleans Hornets selected Chris fourth overall. It didn't take long for Chris to show the team what a great player he was. In fact, no **rookie** scored more points or had more assists in the 2005–2006 season. Chris also led the entire league in steals. It was no surprise when he was named NBA Rookie of the Year.

The season before Chris joined the Hornets, they were one of the NBA's worst teams. With his amazing skills and teamwork, Chris quickly helped turn the team around. As much as he liked to score, he also passed the ball so his teammates could score. Chris was great on defense, too. He was quick and able to get a lot of steals. With Chris leading the way, the Hornets became a winning team. They made the playoffs four times between 2008 and 2011.

Chris's well-timed passes helped his teammates make easy baskets.

Chris (right) driving to the basket during a 2006 game

The Hornets won just 18 games the season before Chris started playing for them. In the 2007–2008 season, with Chris on the team, the Hornets won a team record 56 games and a first-round playoff series.

On to Los Angeles

Chris had grown into one of the NBA's most well-rounded point guards. He could run the offense, score points, and be a strong defender. As a result, many teams wanted him to leave the Hornets and play for them. Chris was ready for a change, too. The Hornets decided to trade him to the Los Angeles Clippers in December 2011.

Chris would have his work cut out for him, however. The Clippers had a long history of losing. In the 41 seasons leading up to the 2011–2012 season, they had made the playoffs only seven times. After Chris joined the team, that losing record changed completely. He led the Clippers to the playoffs in each of his first three seasons.

Chris was selected to play for Team USA at both the 2008 and 2012 Olympics. The team won gold medals both times.

Chris celebrates his 2012 Olympic gold medal.

Chris going up for a basket during a 2014 game

13

An Adopted Hometown

Chris has devoted much of his time to basketball. Yet he has always made time to help out people in need. In August 2005, just before Chris started his first season in the NBA, a terrible storm called Hurricane Katrina hit the Gulf Coast of the United States. The storm caused terrible flooding, especially in New Orleans. Many people in the city died, and thousands of homes were destroyed. Even the Hornets were affected. Chris and his teammates had to play his first two seasons in Oklahoma City because the Hornets' arena was so badly damaged.

Chris wanted to help the people in his new hometown. After Hurricane Katrina, he gave his time and money to rebuild houses throughout the city. Even after Chris left New Orleans, he continued to work with organizations that served the people there.

New Orleans after Hurricane Katrina

Chris takes a break from helping build a house in New Orleans following Hurricane Katrina.

Chris hosts a bowling event each year to raise money to help needy children in New Orleans and Winston-Salem. Athletes and entertainers join top professional bowlers for the event.

Creating a Foundation

Because Chris's family is so important to him, he decided to honor them by starting the CP3 **Foundation** in 2005. The foundation gets its name from Chris's nickname. His father's and brother's nicknames are CP1 and CP2—making Chris CP3. The name also fits because Chris wears #3 on his jersey.

Chris's foundation works with many **charities** in Winston-Salem, New Orleans, Los Angeles, and other cities. Working with these organizations, the foundation provides food, shelter, and other services to people who need help. In addition, the foundation awards **scholarships** each year for two students to attend Wake Forest University.

Chris (far left) works with players during a youth basketball camp he organized in Oklahoma City in 2006.

Every year, the CP3 Foundation hosts a special weekend in Winston-Salem to promote community spirit. The 2008 event included a concert. Chris also ran a youth basketball camp that year.

Chris (left) works with other NBA stars in 2011 to distribute food to those in need in Brooklyn, New York.

Looking Out for Kids

The CP3 Foundation also raises money to help pay for afterschool programs for kids. As children, Chris and C.J. took part in an afterschool program in Winston-Salem, where they made art and played musical instruments. Now Chris wants to make sure other kids have the same opportunities. Sometimes Chris visits kids in these programs and gives them encouragement and advice.

One particular afterschool program that the CP3 Foundation set up is the CP3 AfterSchool Zone at KIPP Central City Primary School in New Orleans. Many students who attend the program come from crime-filled neighborhoods. The CP3 AfterSchool Zone offers the kids a safe place to play sports and games and to do their homework.

To encourage good health, Chris hosts the CP3K Walk for Kids.

To help launch the CP3 AfterSchool Zone in 2010, Chris and Chase Bank donated $1 million.

Chris plays basketball with some kids at the KIPP Central City Primary School in New Orleans.

A Big Honor

In 2013, Chris was one of the biggest stars in the NBA. Yet that didn't stop him from keeping a promise he had made ten years earlier. As the former president of his high school class, Chris was in charge of planning his ten-year high school **reunion**. He spent many hours making phone calls from his home in Los Angeles to plan the event in North Carolina. "It's going to be great," he said at the time.

As his high school friends and NBA teammates know, Chris is extremely generous. Although he has amazing skills on the basketball court, he is never selfish—especially with the ball. He's more than willing to pass it to his fellow players and watch them score. That same attitude applies when he's off the court. Chris helps those who need it most, which makes him an all-around great person and role model.

Chris's wife, Jada, has a history of giving back, too. She sells handmade bracelets and gives the money to charity. In addition, she **donates** prom dresses to girls in need each year.

Chris and his wife, Jada

Chris (left) has earned a spot in the NBA
All-Star Game each year from 2008 to 2014.

The Chris File

Chris is a basketball hero on and off the court. Here are some highlights.

LOS ANGELES
CLIPPERS

- When Chris was three years old, his father bought him and C.J. two toy basketball hoops. Chris's dad then set up a court in the basement and watched his sons go one-on-one.

- Chris still remembers his beloved grandfather. During the national anthem before every game, Chris clutches a copy of a newspaper clipping reporting the death of the man everyone called Papa Chili.

- Chris is a great bowler. As a child, he often joined his father for a day at the bowling alley. He became so good that he once bowled an amazing score of 256 out of a possible 300.

- Chris hosts several free basketball camps and clinics every year for kids in Winston-Salem.

Glossary

assists (uh-SISTS) when a player makes passes that set up his or her teammates to make baskets

charities (CHA-ruh-teez) groups that try to help people in need

donates (DOH-nayts) gives something to a group or cause

draft (DRAFT) an event in which professional teams take turns choosing college athletes to play for them

foundation (foun-DAY-shuhn) an organization that supports or gives money to worthwhile causes

free throws (FREE THROHS) one-point shots awarded to a player if certain fouls have been committed against the player; the shooter takes the shots from the free-throw line with no defender guarding him

layup (LAY-uhp) a shot taken near the basket, usually by playing the ball off the backboard

NBA (EN BEE AY) letters standing for the *National Basketball Association*, the professional men's basketball league in North America

NCAA Tournament (EN SEE AY AY TUR-nuh-muhnt) college basketball's yearly series of games that result in one team becoming the overall champion

offense (AW-fenss) the team that has possession of the ball and is trying to score

playoffs (PLAY-awfs) a series of games played to determine which teams will play in a championship

point guard (POINT GARD) the player whose main jobs are to run plays and pass the ball to teammates who are in a position to score

recruit (ri-KROOT) to persuade an athlete to attend a college and play for its sports team

reunion (ree-YOON-yuhn) an event in which people who have not seen each other for a long time come together

rookie (RUK-ee) a first-year player

scholarships (SKOL-ur-ships) money given to people for education

three-pointer (three-POINT-ur) a long-distance shot that is worth three points

Bibliography

Buckheit, Mary. "CP3 Can Score Big at Hoops and Strikes." *ESPN Page 2* (October 17, 2008).

Paul, Chris. *Long Shot: Never Too Small to Dream Big.* New York: Simon & Schuster (2009).

Pope, John. "New Orleans Hornets' Chris Paul Gives Money to KIPP After-School Program." *The Times-Picayune* (October 28, 2010).

Read More

Bowker, Paul D. *New Orleans Hornets (Inside the NBA).* Edina, MN: ABDO (2012).

Savage, Jeff. *Chris Paul (Amazing Athletes).* Minneapolis, MN: Lerner (2010).

Wilson, Bernie. *Los Angeles Clippers (Inside the NBA).* Edina, MN: ABDO (2012).

Learn More Online

To learn more about Chris Paul and the Los Angeles Clippers, visit **www.bearportpublishing.com/BasketballHeroes**

Index